As I Took My Walk With God

Volume I: How I Stopped Wasting God's Time

Jeremiah Short With Artwork By
Mack Bishop III

To Aunt Florence, I know you're looking over me and I dedicate my first book to you. Rest In Peace.

Foreword

I first met Jeremiah Short just a few years ago at our church in Houston, Texas. Jeremiah had come to live Houston shortly after college and was visiting our College and Young Singles group. Jeremiah soon jumped into the flow of things and joined a young men's Revelation Bible Study already in progress. All participants were required to take a portion of the scripture being studied and present it at the next week's Bible Study. This was not a study for people who just wanted to listen and learn from someone else. It required participation, and Jeremiah actively participated. From those beginnings, Jeremiah and I began to get to know each other. During that process, I had the privilege to see him accept Jesus Christ as personal Lord and Savior and to see him grow in Christ.

As a part of his ongoing spiritual growth and due to his God given talent as a writer, Jeremiah began a daily devotional which he has sent out to friends and family for over three years now.

This book is a compilation of those devotions. Jeremiah is gifted writer, with much to say. He uses daily experiences to teach Bible insights. He speaks to a younger generation that sees and hears things differently than mine did, and perhaps differently than what yours does. Some of his work is edgy, some maybe a bit controversial and some is eternal truth spoken from a new angle with a new voice. But, from whatever life season you are in, if you really want to get inside the head of this new generation and understand their paradigm, their culture, and their issues, then I recommend that you start here.

Love and God Bless,

W. Allen Tate
Elder, Houston Northwest Church

Introduction: My Journey With God

As I took my "Walk With God", I thought my journey with him.

It's been a long winding road. Growing up, I identified as a Christian. But my life didn't look like it. I misused my gift for words to encourage people. I didn't foster good relationships with friends and family. I held grudges, and I didn't take myself or God seriously.

It led to a lifetime of financial instability, hurt and wasted potential.

That all changed when I gave my life over to Christ. I healed from my childhood pain, gained financial stability and started to realize my potential.

If you're a college student who is looking for guidance, young professional dealing with workplace challenges, a person looking to get unstuck, an individual wanting to heal from a rough childhood or a Christian seeking God but doesn't know how to speak to him, my hope is that this book will serve as an encouragement and inspiration.

Join me As I Took My Walk With God.

God Bless, Jeremiah

5/10/15

Sunday's Reflection: "Don't Waste Time"

As I took my "Walk with God", I thought about Ray Lewis' Speech: "Time Don't Stop For Nobody."

Yesterday, I had to wait three hours at an establishment for the owner to return. All I could think about was that I was wasting time.

Reflecting this morning, I realized that I wasted way more time than that at different points in my life. I wasted time playing video games. I wasted time socializing with friends who really weren't friends as a college student. I wasted time dwelling on the past, and the ways that I've been wronged.

While wasting time, I didn't spend enough time thanking God for the blessings that he had bestowed upon me.

I'm blessed with writing, observational and communication skills. Three things that could help me be great occupationally and a better Christian.

I wasted time being mad at the world, which only hurt me.

Don't Waste Time.

God Bless, Jeremiah

05/17/15

Sunday's Reflection: Keep Things In Perspective

As I took my "Walk with God", I thought about how you must keep things in perspective.

This past month, I really didn't want to be around anyone. But I had the itch to do so yesterday.

I ended up not going out anywhere. At a point in the day, though, something shifted. It was like God told me to chill and focus on what I have for you.

I have a few career opportunities coming up and need to mentally prepare myself for the next phase of my life.

I must turn my focus to getting closer to God and furthering my career as a writer while also trying to be the best educator I can be every day.

I'm keeping things in perspective.

God Bless, Jeremiah

05/24/15

Sunday's Reflection: Be Consistent

As I took my "Walk With God", I thought about how you must be consistent.

If you're supposed to get in quiet time every day, then do it. If you're supposed to work out three times a week, then do it. If you're supposed to show up to work on time, then do it. If you're supposed to foster good relationships with people, then do it. If you're supposed to try to get better every day, then do it.

None of us are perfect. But we can strive to be consistent in our behavior and to be the best we can be every day.

It's cool when a few people like and want to hang with you.

But do they value you? More importantly, do you value them?

Would y'all like each other if you knew the true answer to that question?

Finally, the only way we can remain consistent is through a strong relationship with God. Nothing trumps that. Not personal friendships. Not monetary gains. Not professional accolades.

Be Consistent.

God Bless, Jeremiah

05/31/15

Sunday's Reflection: Recommit to God

As I took my "Walk With God", I realized that I must recommit to him.

Over the past few months, I've started to lose my temper more. Something I worked hard to control. I've started to curse a lot more. Something else I've worked hard to eliminate. Also, I haven't been writing much at all--as my focus has been elsewhere.

I haven't been focusing on God. I've been relying on my own thought process and mortal counselors, instead of giving everything to the Creator. And I wondered why I had no peace.

With that said, I need to recommit myself to giving everything over to God. I must be the person that he wants me to be, not what the world thinks I should be.

I'm Recommitting To God.

God Bless, Jeremiah

06/07/15

Sunday's Reflection: Be Thankful.

As I took my "Walk With God", I thought about how you must be thankful.

Be thankful for those people that are in your life and are riding for you. I know all of us want to be Billionaires by 20. But the world doesn't work that way. God places us on a path to get to where we are supposed to be at the right time.

I think about the fact if I had got my stuff together at 22, I wouldn't have several people in my life. I wouldn't know Reggie Harris or Cortez McCraney, two of my best friends. I wouldn't know Bill Roberts, Bill Buckley or Allen Tate, three men I consider spiritual mentors. I definitely wouldn't be at Houston Northwest under the stewardship of Steve Bezner, one of the best pastors I've ever heard. You'll know his name soon. (Pastor Steve is becoming nationally known. Those words proved prophetic.)

Most importantly, I'm thankful to have a strong relationship with God.

Be Thankful for what you have. Because you are not in control...God Is.

God Bless, Jeremiah

06/14/15

Sunday's Reflection: "Pursue Winning Environments"

As I took my "Walk With God", I thought about how we must pursue winning environments.

If there's anything I've learned over the past year, it's that the friends you have and the right environments make a worlds of a difference.

Proverbs speaks of good friends: *"A man of many companions may come to ruin but there is a friend who sticks closer than a brother."*

Truer words were never spoken. My mom once told me not to call some people friends…call them associates.

As I've matured, I've learned to only be around the friends--as you can't trust the associates. They're like leaves. When the season changes, they'll blow away.

Professionally and spiritually--you need to be in situations where people value your presence.

We can't always control our work situations. But we can seek the right ones when the situation presents itself.

Spiritually, if an environment doesn't allow you to grow, then remove yourself from it.

Ultimately, we must put ourselves around the right people and environments to succeed personally, professionally and spiritually.

Environment Is Everything.

God Bless, Jeremiah

06/21/15

Sunday's Reflection: Remain Diligent

As I took my "Walk With God", I thought about how we must remain diligent.

It may have been fresh on my mind--as that was Sunday's Word.

But I thought about the column I forced myself to write on Thursday. I got stuck, but I pushed through and wrote it. It was the first column that I had written in three months.

I realized that the reason that I didn't write in three months was because I didn't stay diligent in my behavior. I never should have stopped writing. No matter what was going on personally and professionally.

But at the time I stopped writing, I wasn't consistent with my quiet time, and it showed up.

I made a vow to get back to writing and remain diligent in all my behaviors.

The way I treat people. The way I write. The way I serve God.

I must remain diligent. I encourage all of you to remain diligent. If you remain diligent, it will reflect in your personal, professional and spiritual life.

God Bless, Jeremiah

06/28/15

Sunday's Reflection: Remain Open

As I took my "Walk With God", I thought about how we must remain open.

This past week, America has experienced many changes. Health Care was upheld. The Confederate Flag is finally being recognized for what it is...a symbol of hate and racism. And same-sex marriage was legalized by the Supreme Court.

Obviously, with all these changes, the country is split along political, ideological, and sadly, spiritual lines.

Yea, I said spiritual lines. Christians have decided that they must draw a line in the sand, not because they're commanded to. But because they must let everyone know where they stand, although it has no spiritual redeeming value.

We shouldn't be that way as Christians.

Christians should ask themselves two important questions.

1. How can a Christian reasonably support the Confederate Flag?

2. How does the legalization of same-sex marriage effect your salvation?

I know change isn't always the easiest thing to take in. But we must.

Christianity must grow and change with the times or get left behind. And for God's sake, support your leaders.

That means supporting President Obama and the Supreme Court. There are Christians who want to subvert the Supreme Court...The SUPREME COURT. The law of the land. Are you serious? I dare you. How arrogant of you? Things didn't go your way. Tough beans. Accept it. We are commanded to support our leaders. Do so.

Just because Gay Marriage is legal...it doesn't mean that everyone is going to marry someone of the same-sex. That's absurd. America isn't slipping into moral decay. It's not. So, check yourselves. It's not our jobs to sort everyone out. That's God's job. We are commanded to love each other. So, why don't we start doing it?

Love your Gay neighbor. Matter of fact, have a convo with them. You won't burst into flames.

I didn't Friday when I talked with a co-worker who told me he was planning on telling his parents he was Gay.

I asked him a few questions. Like if he always had those feelings. He said yes. And he said that his father beat him when he was young because he may have picked up on the fact that he did. He told me that he's done a lot of soul-searching.

At the end of the convo, he thanked me for treating him the same, although he had just came out to me. I was like wow. But I know now that I can be a witness to him.

If I had rebuffed him, I wouldn't have been able to witness to him.

I'm still a Christian and that person's still Gay. But he knows he's welcomed in my religion now.

We must take that approach to every situation. Love on people and remain open. If you close yourself off because of arrogance and bigotry, you're no longer a witness, which God commands us to be.

Remain Open and watch how many people are receptive to you and the God your serve.

God Bless, Jeremiah

07/05/15

Sunday's Reflection: Peace Be Still

As I took my "Walk with God", I thought about the 30's Life Group discussion.

When the disciples were worried about a small storm, Jesus said "Peace Be Still" and it was calmed.

How this relates? I started to have a few car problems. The vehicle got fixed but there were still some electrical issues.

Well...the dealer who I bought the vehicle from called me and asked me to swap it out.

The new vehicle was the same make and model. When I went to pick it up, it was in better condition and probably worth 800-1000 dollars more than the original. I didn't pay anything extra.

God will do it.

I was going through a storm and God said "Peace Be Still."

God Bless, Jeremiah

07/12/15

Sunday's Reflection: Submit Yourself

As I took my "Walk With God", I thought about how you must submit yourself to him.

I suffer with selfishness and sometimes not thinking how small things to me affect others and the fault in it. I'm laid back and don't see the big deal. Well, sometimes things are a big deal and you should apologize for them.

Some of things you view as a little bit of sin is a big sin to God--as there is no sin greater than the next.

I reaffirm that I will be more conscious of my actions and be more thoughtful as to the impact that they have.

I submit myself fully and completely.

Submit Yourself.

God Bless, Jeremiah

07/19/15

Sunday's Reflection: "That's Ok."

As I took my "Walk With God", I thought about a conversation I had with my cousin, Theresa, the other night.

I told her that I have a good relationship with my father--her uncle--but I've never had a man's conversation with him. I want to change that and deepen our relationship.

The more I thought about it on Saturday. I started to question myself: Who am I? I don't really know my father or mother.

So, how can I know myself?

It's a question that I've always asked.

Who am I? I knew I was a kid who did well in school and didn't get in trouble. But I never got my mother's love. So, I always questioned the person I really was.

I always thought: Maybe I'm doing something wrong. My own mom doesn't even love me. I don't care what these other people--teachers and friends have to say about me. My own mom doesn't even love me. That was always a struggle of mine--still is. I mean, I've even thought I could cure and never get that love.

That depression and negative thinking caused me to not excel in school. I mean, what was the point? Not like my mom would care. I was in the "Gifted Program" in my school and straight A student and my mom still didn't love me.

So, why excel?

In addition to that, I never trusted people. I would reject them before they rejected me the way my mom had. So, I never really revealed much about myself to people.

The only two people I felt knew me growing up were Kevin and Demetris. Those guys were always there for me. They got in trouble but were good enough friends to make sure I stayed out of trouble, because they felt I could do something big.

Even with all that hurt and damage I dealt with growing up, I decided to open myself up and attend a predominantly white church, Houston Northwest, in 2013. I was apprehensive at first. It was something new to me. But God released that anxiety. I got "saved" a few months later.

I was getting closer to God, but I felt like I was compromising myself. I was working too hard to make friends. It's supposed to be more organic.

Then I realized one day why it was so hard. One member of the College and Young Singles Ministry I used to belong to said that the children she taught--mostly Black and Hispanic--would never amount to anything.

It was one of the more startling experiences of my life. Even more startling, I saw people--teachers--nod in agreement.

At that moment, I knew that these weren't my type of Christians. We don't serve the same God. My God believes every person has a chance. I knew then that I would eventually leave the Ministry.

Spending time again with some of my brothers in Christ--Cortez, Reggie, Chaney, Dan, Braxton--I saw what young Christians are supposed to look like.

I didn't see it in the Ministry I belonged to.

When I went on a Mission Trip to Puebla, Mexico with *Athletes In Action*, in 2014, I saw it even more. It was a life-changing experience. I saw another world other than my own and got to meet so many great men. Clint Mahan. Matt Spitz. Brandon Richardson. Chris Couch. Tyler Warner. Chris Davis.

They thought I was ok. It made me put away my thoughts of wanting to change things about myself.

Eventually, after much counsel and prayer, I left the *CYS* Ministry.

I focused on learning from Steve Bezner and pouring into the Children's Ministry.

A weight was lifted off my shoulders. Some of those demons are still there, but I'm working to get past them and find myself.

I'm a fast talker, opinionated, straight-forward and my "approach" isn't always the best.
But I love my babies--HNW and Club Rewind. I'm an intellectual who loves the world and wants to see it get better.

First and foremost, that I'm a child of God.

And "That's Ok."

God Bless, Jeremiah

07/26/15

Sunday's Reflection: "Deal With Your Demons"

As I took my "Walk With God", I thought a lot about last week's Sunday's Reflection and about personal responsibility.

In writing that reflection, a demon was released from me. I don't tell many people about what I dealt with growing up or how it still affects me. But it was freeing. I saw myself starting to do things I wouldn't do before because I feared rejection.

We all have demons, but we can't let them rule us and determine our movements.

It's fair to acknowledge those issues, but they aren't excuses. We must push to overcome them and grow as Christians.

We go through those things to strengthen our faith. God will never put more on you than you can bear. Never forget that. I had a lot of things happen over the course of the past year. But I'm still here and professing the name of Christ.

Deal With Your Demons.

God Bless, Jeremiah

08/02/15

Sunday's Reflection: "Oh Ok God"

As I took my "Walk with God", I was being thankful for the place I was in my life.

For most of my adult life, I was broken, damaged and trying to find myself. But over the past year, God has worked in my life. I see myself maturing personally, professionally and spiritually.

There's was a time when I was disappointed, because I hadn't accomplished much. I was in the "Gifted" program growing up.

Due to that "label", I was destined to be a superstar by 20, right?

That's not what God wanted, though. He wanted to reveal some things to me and bring some people into my life.

Examples

1. When I was in college, I went through a rough time and lost weight. But I started writing to get things off my chest and one of my gifts was revealed to me: exhortation.

2. I was unemployed and started working as a Para and with Club Rewind. I discovered that I loved working with children. As I gained stability, I developed as a person and professional.

I understand now that God put me through everything he did to make me a man who would be a soldier for Christ. I've met so many people that wouldn't have met if I had got myself together earlier.

I couldn't imagine not having Allen Tate, Bill Roberts, Dobie Weise, Cortez McCraney, Bill Buckley, Reggie Harris, Jamar Chaney, Roderick Cox, Ann Scott, Matt Geiss, Susan McHenry, Jill Gentry Roberts and all the great men of AIA in my life.

If I had got it together at 20, I wouldn't know most of them.

I'm thankful to God for bringing through the storm and into the light.

Next time I go through a trial, instead of complaining, I'm going to say…Oh Ok God.

God Bless, Jeremiah

08/09/15

Sunday's Reflection: "Keep The Faith"

As I took my "Walk With God", I thought about how you must keep the faith.

I've learned to rely on God with most things, but when things don't go my way, I rest to much on my own devices.

In 1 Peter 5:6-7, he writes: *"Therefore, humble yourselves under the mighty hand of God, that He may exalt you at the proper time, casting all your anxiety on Him, because He cares for you."*

Last Night, I realized that I must put my anxieties aside and rely on the Creator.

You can't put your faith in yourself or other people. One of the best words of wisdom I've ever heard is from Pastor Lee Brand Jr.: "Never put your faith in people (or yourself) ...they will always disappoint you."

And he's right.

How can we trust other people? You can't even trust yourself to always make the right decision.

All we can do is Keep the Faith.

God Bless, Jeremiah

08/16/15

Sunday's Reflection: Admit Your Weaknesses

As I took my "Walk With God", I thought about how you must admit your weaknesses.

I have three.

1. When I'm frustrated, I lose my temper way too much.
2. I don't respect authority enough.
3. I'm not patient enough.

2 Corinthians states: *"For the sake of Christ, then, I am content with weaknesses, insults, hardships, persecutions, and calamities. For when I am weak, then I am strong."*

In a nutshell, we all are weak or have weaknesses, that's what makes us who we are and allows us to be a witness.

With me, every issue that I've had this year...It's been because I lost my temper. And I'm glad God has revealed that to me. Now, I can assess how I can stay calm and settle issues more diplomatically.

We are commanded to respect authority. But I don't always respect it, although I do most of the time. I must challenge myself to go along with a superior, even when I don't agree.

Personality wise, I'm an introvert, but I have a takeover gene in me. I grew up around Type A people: Twanda, Florence, Allean and Berto. So, I always took a step back.

But now I'm faced with situations where I'm taking over way too much. I'm becoming the Type A person I rebelled against most of my life.

I must work to establish a balance. That's been made easier, though, because I've admitted my weaknesses.

God Bless, Jeremiah

08/23/15

Sunday's Reflection: "Let Go and Let God"

As I took my "Walk With God", I thought about how you must "Let Go and Let God."

I'm reminded of what Paul wrote in 2 Corinthians 4:16-18: *"Therefore, we do not lose heart, but though our outer man is decaying, yet our inner man is being renewed day by day. For momentary, light affliction is producing for us an eternal weight of glory far beyond all comparison, while we look not at the things which are seen, but at the things which are not seen; for the things which are seen are temporal, but the things which are not seen are eternal."*

In simple terms, what doesn't kill you will make you stronger.

I went through a tough time in college once and started writing and my gift was revealed. I got teased in school. It made me more empathetic to others plight. I made several mistakes as an adult. I can steer those younger than me away from those same mistakes.

God puts up certain obstacles for a reason. He wants to open our eyes and strengthen us. He never gives you more than you can handle. That doesn't mean you have to do it alone, though.

I struggle with relying on God when things don't go my way. I'm thinking, I'm Jeremiah, I'll show that person or persons. But no. I should be saying: Let God handle it. LET God handle it. But that's easier said than done--especially when you're upset.

Let Go and Let God.

God Bless, Jeremiah

08/30/15

Sunday's Reflection: "Don't Fight God"

As I took my "Walk with God", I thought about how I don't need to fight him. Why do I say that?

I was in a situation in one of my two jobs last year where I had to leave. I went through months of depression. Even worse, I didn't have a lot of people I could talk to about it. Once I did, I started to come out of my funk.

Wednesday evening, before I left, I asked my supervisor if we had a meeting and did I need to stay. My supervisor told me that basically that we did, but it's nothing I need to be talked to about. I was like wait…what? I couldn't sneeze wrong without being told something was wrong with what I was doing last year. Same stuff.

Friday, my manager told me I did a "good job." I'm not big on "affirmation." But it did feel pretty good to hear that.

At that moment, I told God: I see why you put me through what you did and led me to this situation.

1 Peter 5:6-7: "Therefore humble yourselves under the mighty hand of God, that He may exalt you at the proper time, casting all your anxiety on Him, because He cares for you."

God did humble me over the past few months and year. But now I feel he's about to walk me into miracle territory.

Don't Fight God.

God Bless, Jeremiah

09/06/15

Sunday's Reflection: "Take It To God"

As I took "Walk With God", I thought about how we must take it to God.

On Friday, God revealed the mortal people who I can trust and revealed to me that I should put my faith in him.

A couple of weeks ago, I wrote a Reflection detailing how I needed to rely on God, instead of my own devices.

This week, God tested me and put me in position to trust in him. A co-worker misinterpreted an interaction, which caused an issue.

Instead of relying on my own devices, I took it to God.

In the past, when I faced trials, I relied on me. Now, I process, take counsel and take it to God.

God Bless, Jeremiah

09/13/15

Sunday's Reflection: "Put Yourself In Other's Shoes"

As I took my "Walk With God", I thought about how you must put yourself in others shoes.

Last week, I wrote about a work issue and that I had to take to God.

I discovered that the crux of a disagreement was miscommunication.

What I discovered was that my co-worker and I were saying the same thing…just in a different way.

As the conversation proceeded, I was like, wow, how many situations would have gone differently if I had been more conscious of how I talk and respond to others?

I'm serious-minded person who doesn't always take time getting to know people. And due to that, I have several "blind spots."

After this week, I have one less blind spot. I aim to thrive personally, professionally and spiritually in any situation or environment.

If I'm around someone who is assertive, I know I'll be fine. I don't mix well with passive people. But I must adapt to those who are Type B, not Type A.

To end, I must be conscious of my behavior and put myself in other's shoes.

God Bless, Jeremiah

09/20/15

Sunday's Reflection: Wait On God

As I took my "Walk With God", I thought how you must wait on God.

This week, I got to train someone for the first time. I've helped people and given advice before but never trained anyone. I considered it a tremendous honor. I just had to stop and thank God for bringing everything full circle.

God certainly tested me in the past year. I lost my Aunt Florence who I loved more than life itself. I dealt with racism at work and on the home front. I got lied on at work. I left my church group. My Dwell Group split apart twice. And I finally dealt with some childhood demons.

Through it all, God has been my saving Grace.

My eyes have been open to so much. I have peace in my life.

After every trial, God has put me in better situations. There were times when I went: Why God?

But now, I'm like: I see Why.

I've been meditating on Romans 12:9-21: *Let love be genuine. Abhor what is evil, hold fast to what is good. Love one another with brotherly affection. Outdo one another in showing honor. Do not be slothful in zeal, be fervent in spirit, serve the Lord. Rejoice in hope, be patient in tribulation, be constant in prayer. Contribute to the needs of saints and seek to show hospitality.*

Bless those who persecute you; bless and do not curse them. Rejoice with those who rejoice, weep with those who weep. Live in harmony with one another. Do not be haughty, but associate with the lowly. Never be wise in your own sight. Repay no one evil for evil, but give thought to do what is honorable in the sight of all. If possible, so far as it depends on you, live peaceably with all. Beloved, never avenge yourselves, but leave it to the wrath of God, for it is written, Vengeance is mine, I will repay, says the Lord.

To the contrary, if your enemy is hungry, feed him; if he is thirsty, give him something to drink; for by so doing you will heap burning coals on his head. Do not be overcome by evil, but overcome evil with good."

I'm only beginning the 40-Day challenge to read these verses every day and meditate on them. But it has changed my perspective. All I'm thinking now is "Abhor what is Evil" and "Wait On God."

God Bless, Jeremiah

09/27/15

Sunday's Reflection: "Hurt People…Hurt People"

As I took my "Walk With God", I thought about a conversation that I had with one of my kids on Friday.

I asked the her why she said something mean to another student. The student told me it was because another student was mean to her, and she didn't know how to display her frustration other than by taking it out on someone else.

The student apologized to the other student.

How this relates?

Saturday morning, I had a conversation with a mentor. We talked about race in America and how people should understand each other better.

He shared that after some black males accosted him without provocation, he was racist for a time period or at least felt that he was.

Then I shared with him that due to recent and past encounters, I've had my own issues with White males.

The moral: An eight-year old child, 30-year old black man and 60-year old white man are engaging in the same behavior.

Hurting people because someone hurt them.

That's not how Christianity works. We're called to love on everyone and overlook offenses. If we don't, we perpetuate a vicious cycle that leads to the brokenness that we have in the world.

We must take that "log" out our own eye and do what Christ calls us to do: Love on each other, not hurt each other.

Hurt People…Hurt People.

God Bless, Jeremiah

09/29/15

Tuesday's Reflection: "What's The Alternative?"

I was reflecting on a 30's life group conversation. We were talking about "Working While You Worship."

I shared that I have little free time and must sit in the house Saturday to recharge the batteries from the week.

But then I asked: What's the alternative?

I struggled through most of my 20's with finding stable work. I worked at a newspaper right out of college, a chicken plant, farm store, substituted, a convenience store, cleaned Davis-Wade Stadium while working on a Radio Show that talked about the games going on in it, did security and finally when I got a job that I thought was stable…lost that expectantly, too.

All the while, I dealt with a variety of issues.

I dealt with lack of drive, purpose and depression. If it wasn't for Allen Tate and The Furter's, a South African family, whom allowed me to stay with them until I got on my feet, I would have been homeless.

Eventually, I got two jobs in the Cy-Fair school district. Early in the first year as a teacher, I lost my Aunt Florence, who was a second mother to me. I told others to be strong, but I was barely holding it together myself.

The best way to honor her memory was to keep pushing. If she can sit up in a chair until God called her home, I can at least take my butt to work and not complain.

So, what's the alternative? Living without God and being broken or living with him and having peace and joy.

I know which one I choose. *God Bless, Jeremiah*

10/04/15

Sunday's Reflection: "Press Pause"

As I took my "Walk With God", I thought about how you must press pause.

This week, I had two professional situations where I was required to take a step back.

First Situation: I felt that I needed more administrative support in a and was prepared to ask for it. Then as I got to work, I decided to try to make a small change with something I was doing. I made the strategic change, and it worked.

Second Situation: Someone felt I was rude in an interaction. Nothing major. But said I was rude nonetheless. I'm a black male in America. You kind of get use to this type of stuff. But I got an opportunity to speak to the person and have a conversation. They explained why they felt I did something wrong. I was like, oh ok and told them I didn't mean in that way and apologized.

Third Situation: I had a conversation with someone. Instead of dismissing everything that they said, I listened to what they had to say. When they revealed what they had a problem with, it made sense.

In all those situations, others may have been wrong or "tripping", but I was wrong, too.

If we hope to grow, we must "Press Pause."

God Bless, Jeremiah

10/11/15

Sunday's Reflection: "Hold A High Standard"

As I took my "Walk With God", I thought about James 2:14-18: *"What good is it, my brothers, if someone says he has faith but does not have works? Can that faith save him? If a brother or sister is poorly clothed and lacking in daily food, and one of you says to them, "Go in peace, be warmed and filled," without giving them the things needed for the body, what good is that? So also faith by itself, if it does not have works, is dead. But someone will say, "You have faith and I have works. Show me your faith apart from your works, and I will show you my faith by my works."*

In simpler terms, what's truly in your heart?

You can't be one way in public and another in private. You can't say that you're not a racist because the one black friend you have says what you're doing is cool. Then go support a cop killing an unarmed black kid. Not congruent.

You can't say that no sin is greater than the next. Then look all downtrodden when someone mentions the gay co-worker but at the same time defend Josh Duggar's sins. Both sins should be judged equally.

You can't say you have a giving heart but struggle with giving to the homeless--citing examples of those who are duplicitous while pan handling. We're not supposed to "bat a thousand."

You can't say that you're a Christian and show up work late every day and be lazy while there. We're commanded to strive for excellence in every arena. If you love God, people should "see it" through your faith and actions. That means at work, the store or a restaurant.

Christians must be accountable and "Hold Themselves to a Higher Standard."

God Bless, Jeremiah

10/18/15

Sunday's Reflection: "My Why"

As I took my "Walk With God, I thought about my Why.

This past weekend, I returned home and got a chance to see my friends, alma mater, Mississippi State, play live and got to spend time with my family.

All I could think about was this is what I do it for. It…walking the path of righteousness and striving for Greatness.

I think about my two best friends--Demetris and Kevin.

Demetris and I haven't had an argument in the 20 years that we've known each other. He's the same person who got up early in high school to pick me up to go to school and picks up the phone at 3 a.m. when I have an issue.

Kevin, who's exactly a month younger than me (Inside Joke), has had his troubles. Amid those troubles, he's always been a Great friend.

For example, he kept me out of trouble, because he thought I had a chance to do something big. I don't think he thought it'd take 20 years, though.

I think about Bill Buckley, one of my spiritual mentors, and how much I appreciate his mentorship.

I think about my family. My dad, Aunt Linda, grandma, Eva Kate and how they've always been there for me.

I want to make them proud. I want them to say that's my friend. That's my nephew. That's my son. That's my Grandson. He's making a difference in the world.

They're "My Why." *God Bless, Jeremiah*

10/25/15

Sunday's Reflection: "It's Time"

I wasn't able to take a "Walk With God" this morning (inclement weather), but I was able to reflect on the week and what God had revealed to me.

Friday, I had a conversation with co-worker. He told me that it was time for me to get on "Team 1."

I was like, nah, I'm good. I like not being stressed going to my other job.

Then I found out at my other job that we'd lost one of our best leaders to another school. So, there would be more on me. I wasn't really feeling that, either.

Saturday morning, I caught myself: "Jeremiah, you're being real average right now. You're in position to be great. But you're content with being average."

I had an opportunity to step up at both jobs and gain my certification in Special Education by the end of the next week.

God was setting me up for Greatness, but I was being average.

God's saying: It's Time.

I'm saying: I'm not ready.

God's saying: It's Time.

After checking myself, I said: It's Time, It's Time, It's TIME…

God Bless, Jeremiah

11/01/15

Sunday's Reflection: "It Was Time"

As I took my "Walk With God", I thought about how "It Was Time."

Last week, I talked about how I was thinking average and fighting God when he wanted Greatness for me.

This week, he elevated me. I was placed in a different room at my school…a more challenging room where I'll get a chance to earn "Team 1" status.

I settled into a role of having more responsibility at my other job, as well.

I passed my "Special Education" exam, too. It was an awesome feeling. While my plan is to teach Elementary, I'm one step closer to gaining my certification.

I wasn't even confident that I had passed the test--considering that I barely got to the testing center on time due to traffic, even after leaving early. I was on edge the first 30 questions. Then I prayed for God to relax my mind, and he did.

He was always in control, though. I didn't have a reason to be nervous.

It was Time for me. It can be Time for you, too.

Call on him. Talk to him. Praise him.

God Bless, Jeremiah

11/08/15

Sunday's Reflection: "Strive For Balance"

As I took my "Walk With God", I thought about how you must strive for balance.

Christians are commanded to be good in all areas.

You must be diligent at work. You must strive for excellence but minister to people through your actions and words. With your friends, you must be a light.

In your family dynamic, if no one is a Christian, you must gracefully attempt to steer them toward God.

When you're leading a family, God must come first. Otherwise, there's no foundation. And it will all crumble.

How do we get that balance?

First, get in the Word. That's a starter.

Learn yourself personally, professionally and spiritually. What are your strengths? Weaknesses?

Ask yourself honest questions: Do you have a temper? Do you struggle with alcohol? Or drugs? Or porn?

Once you assess those strengths and weaknesses, seek counsel- -mortal and spiritual to accentuate the strengths and develop the weaknesses.

It's helped me.

I know my weaknesses. I have lust issues, a bit of a temper, don't trust people. I know I can be to assertive, abrasive and step on toes.

I know my strengths, too. I'm disciplined, reliable and a natural leader.

To get true balance, though, you must let God direct your steps.

God Bless, Jeremiah

11/15/15

Sunday's Reflection: "Conquer Your Demons"

As I took my "Walk With God", I thought about how you must conquer your demons.

Earlier this week, someone caught me off guard with a statement that upset me. I engaged in a back-n-forth with the person and started to feel the anger boiling up in me.

But a voice told me to "Stop."

I did.

During a mediation, the other person continued to get angry, and I calmly explained the situation. And due to the calmer approach, it worked out in my favor.

That's not how I've always handled things. There's biblical instruction that I should have followed in the past.

Matthew 18:15-17: *"If your brother sins against you, go and tell him his fault, between you and him alone. If he listens to you, you have gained your brother. But if he does not listen, take one or two others along with you, that every charge may be established by the evidence of two or three witnesses. If he refuses to listen to them, tell it to the church. And if he refuses to listen even to the church, let him be to you as a Gentile and a tax collector."*

It's one situation. But it did feel different.

It was like God was saying: "Son, don't give into your weakness (Demon). And I didn't.

I'll always have to fight that demon and other ones. But I know how to fight them now.

We all have demons. Take them to God and see how fast you conquer them.

God Bless, Jeremiah

11/22/15

Sunday's Reflection: "Speak Life, Not Death"

As I took my "Walk With God", I thought about how you must speak life, not death.

This week, I made some negative comments that caused immense damage, and I had to clean it up.

During that process, I reminded myself that God has blessed me with the spiritual gift of exhortation. I've always had the ability to build up others and calm the waters.

While I can uplift others, I can tear them down, as well. And I've misused it at times.

God didn't bless me with the ability to exhort because he wanted me to speak death. He blessed me with that gift, so I could encourage those who are down and spread his everlasting love.

Jesus said it best in Matthew 15:11: *"It is not what goes into the mouth that defiles a person, but what comes out of the mouth; this defiles a person."*

I defiled myself. But I recognize it. And now I must repent.

To go with that, I must meditate on Matthew 15:11 before I speak. That doesn't mean I shouldn't hold people accountable.

Before I open my mouth, though, I must ask myself: Is this speaking life into the situation?

I encourage you to do the same.

Speak Life, Not Death

God Bless, Jeremiah

11/29/15

Sunday's Reflection: "An Ode To Flo"

As I took my "Walk With God", I thought about my Aunt Florence.

I got to thinking about her all week and thought about how I never grieved for her. I didn't know how to.

Then I watch the movie "Creed."

In the movie, Rocky talks to his deceased wife at her grave. It gave me an idea. I need to write a letter to Flo.

So, excuse me as I take this reflection to talk to her.

Hey Flo,

First, I love and miss you. I'm doing well. I had some rough times during my first year of teaching. But I pushed through. God revealed so much to me. I became a better man and Christian.

Things are starting to look up, though. I covered another NCAA tournament and got to interview Coach K. I'm in a Teacher Certification program. I'm joining the family business. I had the honor of attending the NSSA Hall of Fame Weekend. I'm going on another mission trip in May. And I now have my own radio show. It's called "The Shop With J.Short."

Most importantly, I'm getting in the word daily and growing as a Christian.

You're still my heart. I miss you every day. I'm looking forward to our next talk.

God Bless, Jeremiah

12/06/15

Sunday's Reflection: "He's Not Through With Us"

As I took my "Walk With God", I thought about how he's not through with us."

Recently, I've been excited about my internet radio show: "The Shop With J.Short." The first recording went great. This week, everything that could go wrong went wrong. I was disappointed.

But I didn't stay disappointed for long. Listening to the advice of an administrator, I decided to turn that negative into a positive. Even though things didn't go perfectly, I know what areas I can correct to make the podcast Great.

It's a perfect allegory to Christian life. God puts you through trials for you grow and become stronger.

I know from personal experience. I went through a bad experience my fourth year in college. I lost 50 pounds and failed most of my classes.

What else happened that year? I started to write for therapeutic reasons. And now, I'm able to lift others up with my writing.

Last year, I went through some trials professionally and interpersonally.

What happen as a result? I became a better Christian.

I still make mistakes, but my steps are now guarded by God.

When things happen now, I go: Ooohhhh, God's about to reveal something new to me.

He's not through with me. And he's not through with you. Trust in him. Talk to him. Trust the process of becoming a better Christian.

He's Not Through With Us.

God Bless, Jeremiah

12/13/15

Sunday's Reflection: "Joy In Knowing My Purpose"

As I took my "Walk With God", I thought about a video from Eric Thomas: "Know Your Core."

He spoke our purpose. It's something I often think about.

What's my purpose?

The people who are encouraged by my Sunday Reflections. The Chilton's who can spend more time with their family, because I show up every Sunday. The friends who ask me to pray for them. The people who I'm able to reach with my writing. And the kids who pay attention to my every move.

I thank the Lord for equipping me with the tools to reach all those people.

How did he do that? He exposed me to several environments.

I've attended schools and churches that are predominantly Black and White. So, I've seen both worlds.

One side of my family is blue collar. The other is white collar. Due to that, I have work ethic and good leadership skills.

I went on a Mission Trip and saw how another culture lived in their element. And I'm exposed to new sub-cultures living in a multi-ethnic city. I grow every day from it.

Even with all those reasons to get up, I have tough days. I miss home. My friends. My family.

And I have some lonely days.

Friday, though, all that worry was wiped away.

I was on the playground supervising my Club Rewind kids, and I found myself smiling…just smiling.

At that moment, I realized that I was happy about my place in life and have "Joy In My Purpose."

God Bless, Jeremiah

12/20/15

Sunday's Reflection: "The Next Chapter"

As I took my "Walk With God", I thought about the next chapter…teaching.

Finishing my coursework and passing the Core test is the only obstacle in the way.

I host a radio show, too.

With that show, my vision of meshing teaching with my journalist endeavors is becoming a reality. There's pressure that comes with both.

As a teacher, you'll must deal with kids, parents and administrators. As a journalist, you must deal with fans, producers and editors. Criticism will hit you from all fronts.

Despite the pressure that comes with both roles, it's what I wanted.

When I quit doing security almost three years ago, I wanted more, and God gave me more.

Why complain?

Every week, I'm reminded that God is moving in my life.

For example, I got a gift card from one of my kids for Christmas. The next morning, I saw that one of my automated bill payments was 25 dollars more than usual because of a rate change. How much the gift card was for? 25 dollars.

I'm excited about where I'm at, but I'm ready to for "The Next Chapter."

God Bless, Jeremiah

12/27/15

Sunday's Reflection: "It's Just A Window"

As I took my "Walk With God", I thought how it's just a window.

Tuesday, I was rushing to get to my room--as I had a limited time to prepare for my podcast that started in two hours. But as I entered the room, I saw glass on the ground. I thought the globe in the ceiling had fallen. But it hadn't. Then I realized that my window had a hole in it…strange.

I was a little weirded out and disheveled for about 30 minutes. I called the owner and let him know what happened. I had to get it together. I had a podcast to get ready for.

The owner came and patched up the window. The podcast went well. I prayed and talked to God before I went to sleep.

The next day, God gave me tremendous focus to complete my coursework and study for my Core Test.

I realized that I shouldn't be worried about some broken window. I've had several of them in my life that I didn't overcome.

The pressure to be great was my biggest broken window. I felt I was criticized at 15 like I was 30 for my decision making. I didn't want to be great yet. It took years to reach that point.

I'm there now.

A word of advice: Next time, when you have a broken window, realize that "It's Just A Window."

God Bless, Jeremiah

01/03/16

Sunday's Reflection: "The Little Things"

As I took my "Walk With God", I thought about the little things.

Tuesday, as I left work, one of my kids came to the window and waved. It really hit me. I didn't say good bye to the kids. I normally do , but I was so focused on getting home and preparing for my podcast…Selfish!!!

Those little things matter, though. Kids make you realize that more than anything. They value you being there every day, playing a board game with them or talking to them when they have a problem.

It's an allegory to Christian life.

The little things add up to make the whole Christian. Praying, talking to God, encouraging others, a kind word, being considerate (Ex: Putting the buggy back at Wal-Mart.), fellowshipping (not socializing) and getting in the Word…DAILY.

It's not all about works.

Pastor Lee Brand Jr. of Bethel in Starkville, Mississippi once said this, though: "You might tell your wife you love her. But you have to show her every once in a while."

It's the same with God.

How do you show him that you love him? You show him by doing the little things. We like to focus on the big stuff. Praying publicly. Attending church. Going to a bible study.

Those are the things people see. What are you doing when they aren't watching you? That's what important.

Do the little things.

God Bless, Jeremiah

01/10/16

Sunday's Reflection: "The Box"

As I took my "Walk With God" I thought about "The Box."

On Monday, one of my kids made me an origami box. The next day, I had my Core EC-6 test to get certified.

Before I entered the building, I looked at The Box for motivation—as a reminder of who I do it for.

I got the results Friday…Passed!!!

It took me a while to get to this point. I went through a lot of struggles after college. I had a myriad of odd jobs trying to survive. No stability. All I did was sulk over a missed opportunity after college. When I moved to Houston, I worked security for two years.

There was a point, though, where I realized I wanted more. So, I quit.

I got that first professional job, but I lost it unexpectantly after two months…bummer. Then I got a job as a Life Skills Aide at The Carlton Center and Club Rewind Team Leader. Things came into focus. I started to grow personally, professionally and spiritually.

Reflecting on what I'm positioned to do now, I thought of a statement from my best friend, Kevin. He told me that he kept me out of trouble growing up, because he thought I could do something big.

At the time, it didn't even resonate with me. Now it does. I appreciate him for seeing something in me when I didn't see something in myself.

His belief in me is another reminder of what I do it for. I do it for those who believed in me.

It's not the end of my journey. I must become a great, not good teacher. I must become a great, not good writer and radio host.

That's what I was meant to do and what those who believed in me thought I could do.

I'll keep that box as a reminder of that.

God Bless, Jeremiah

01/17/16

Sunday's Reflection: "Be The Fruit You Want To See"

As I took my "Walk With God", I thought about you must be the fruit you want to see.

Monday, someone slighted me. I didn't blow up or fuss about it. But I did seek counsel. I was advised that I should respond correctly to the slight.

Thankfully, it was sorted out quickly.

The week was still a little funky, though. I felt out of place all week. I didn't sleep well. My kids were shaky. They were a 6 or 7 when I expect them to be a 9 or 10. Anything less is unacceptable.

Mid-week, I was thinking: Let's just get it over with and get to this awesome three-day weekend.

But Thursday, I had to check myself. I'm all about establishing a positive and winning environment, but I'm thinking negatively.

Friday, I got up early and spent 30 minutes in the Word, instead of 15. My routine was smooth until school started.

Something amazing happened: The day went great. We aced our classroom observation, and my kids acted like they had some sense at Club Rewind. ☺

What came to my mind? A line from one of my accountability partners: "Be the Fruit you want to See."

What does that mean? Try to inspire the change you want to see.

If no one in your group of friends encourages the others, why don't you encourage? If you're a teacher and the other teachers don't care enough, why don't you care more? If you want to see more Godly behavior in your family, then let God be reflected in your actions and behaviors.

You'll be amazed how the whole temperature, tone and culture of situations will change more times than not.

For that to happen, though, you must "Be the Fruit you want to See."

God Bless, Jeremiah

01/24/16

Sunday's Reflection: "Understand Your Presence"

As I took my "Walk With God," I thought about a conversation I had with my cousin Cyrus, who is 6'9, the previous week.

Cyrus told me that he's finally starting to realize his presence when he walks in the room.

I shared with him how I came to a similar realization based off a small interaction.

The Interaction

I was walking down the hall and some teachers were discussing something, and I chimed in. I was behind the teacher, and the volume of my voice startled her.

I apologized.

Then I thought: Man, if she had that reaction when I'm talking regular, I can only imagine how she might feel if I was upset and raised my voice.

After we talked about both our realizations, we discussed how we both wished that we were doing a little better when my Aunt Florence passed away.

But I told him that we got it together now…like every other person in the family has started to do.

Friday, I talked to a child that's used to be in Club Rewind. I asked if she was still in the program. She said no, but at least I get to see "you." (Her mother had lost her job.)

It touched me that I was so important her. She was never in my group. All I did was make her smile one day. It was just another confirmation of why God took me on the path that he has the past couple of years.

The next day, at a Club-Rewind training, I had a chance to see Dr. Adolph Brown, a phenomenal speaker and educator, speak.

As an educator, his speech will always stick with me. He told us to be mindful of how we present ourselves to the kids.

Girls don't dress so sexy. What does that say about you?

Guys wear your pants correctly and take off your hat when you walk in the building.

How do all these things tie into a Christian message? It matters how you carry yourself, how you speak and how you handle situations.

I'll ask a question: If someone walked in room, could they tell you were a Christian just by observing you?

As Christians, we know how important God's presence is in our lives.

Why don't we let his light show through our actions?

That's a true Christian Witness.

Understand Your Presence.

I leave you with two things.

1. Is your presence a negative or positive one?

2. Think about whose presence you value. Thank them today or at some point this week.

God Bless, Jeremiah

01/31/16

Sunday's Reflection: "Count Your Blessings"

As I took my "Walk With God", I thought about how you must count your blessings.

Monday, my nephew, Christopher Daniels, had a pretty good basketball game. I put together a highlight tape that went semi-viral…11,000 views.

Yea, my nephew's a baller. You know what he is, too, a scholar-athlete. He got invited to the National Junior Honor Society.

I remember having a dream that my sister was pregnant with my nephew. The part I never told was that, in the dream, she lost the child. What's spooky is that I had another relative lose a child at the six-month mark that my sister lost her child in the dream. I found this out years after the dream.

Maybe God was trying to tell me something.

I'm thankful that God is still blessing my family. They've come a long way since my mom and her four sisters slept on the same bed as children. They didn't let that deter them from becoming successful.

Out of that house, three of them got a four-year college degree with a fourth on the way in the next year. Two have a Master's degree. Two are business owners.

Their children were blessed, too. There are five college graduates (Two with Master's), three college athletes, a journalist, a coach and two soldiers.

We've been blessed.

At one point, I thought we'd lose that blessing. Jealous-hearted behavior permeated the family, people weren't good stewards of their money, and we didn't treat each other or others outside the family the right way.

But over the past few years, the tone in the family has shifted. We're more supportive of each other, becoming financially healthy and engaging in the right habits.

My nephew has a blueprint for success. He's surrounded by educators, servicemen and entrepreneurs.

Most importantly, he lives in a Christ-centered household. I love the prayer circle my brother-in-law leads when I visit my sister. That's what I feel is the future of our family.

Giving God his Glory in every arena. That's how you "Count Your Blessings."

I leave you with two things.

1. What are you thankful for?

2. Is anyone thankful for you?

God Bless, Jeremiah

02/07/16

Sunday's Reflection: "Who Do YOU Represent?"

As I took my "Walk With God" this morning, I thought of a question asked during a work meeting: Who do you represent?

Deep, right?

It was a good question to see where everyone's heart was it. There were some encouraging answers.

To me, it was easy. God. Family. Kids.

Here's why.

I'm going to start with why I represent my family.

I represent my family, because I'm a blend of both. I'm a fast-talker, strong-willed, natural leader like my mom's side of the family. I get my warm, overprotective and level-headed nature from my dad's side. I got my work ethic from both.

I take pride in being Eva Kate's, my dad's mother, grandson. There's something to that. I still remember my Grandma telling me that her father, my great-grandfather, told them as kids to never pick at nobody, meddle anybody and help people if you can. Simple but great advice. I live by it.

Why I represent my babies?

Simple: They need me, and I need them.

When I first started working with kids about two years ago, I had never really worked with kids. I had to figure it out. But eventually, I started to like working with them, and now I love it.

Working with kids, you don't have to think. They either like you or they don't. I love getting my little notes and pictures. It brightens my day.

I had a moment this week where I really thought about it.

I was talking with one of my kids and asked her if her dad had blonde hair since her mom had dark hair. She said no. He has brown hair.

Then she shared: We don't talk about him much…Sad!!!

Her statement struck me…Why?

I realized that I might be the only consistent, male presence in her life. I need to take it seriously.

Most importantly, I represent God. I'm filled with his spirit. It must show with every move I make. I'll make mistakes. But I must aim to correct them and be accountable. He expects nothing else.

If I represent him, then I'll be a blessing to my family and my babies.

I leave you with two things.

1. Who do YOU represent?

2. Would they be proud of you?

God Bless, Jeremiah

02/14/16

Sunday's Reflection: "Iron Sharpens Iron"

As I took my "Walk With God", I thought about how "iron sharpens iron."

I love where I'm at right now. I had a rough year last year. But things are better now. Someone even told me I'm in my "zone."

I guess I am. It's not all me, though.

My environment has changed. I'm working and learning from one of the best teachers and paras at The Carlton Center. My Club Rewind environment is awesome. I'm learning from the teachers there, and I'm blessed to have the best manager in the program, who has mentored me and forced me to grow.

I have a solid squad.

Reggie encourages me every day. It's inspiring to watch him inspire people. It's crazy how we became friends.

Check this out: He was friends with my older brother when they were kids. He coached my little brother. And then we finally had a chance to hang out once and been tight ever since.

Cortez inspires me because he loves people so much. One night, as we left the movies, he struck up conversation with someone. I asked if he knew the guy. He said, nah, I just started talking to him. It was the coolest thing. But that's Tez.

Jamar or "Chaney" inspires me because he's always trying to encourage people, too. He lives for his family. I love to see that. He was a star in college and played NFL ball. You never would guess it through by his humble attitude.

Rod, who I met a few years ago while we were co-workers, has been one of the more consistent people in life. I remember going to a Mississippi State game at NRG and not having money. He gave me money to get something to eat. I'll never forget it.

Dez inspires me, because he was always focused growing up. I remember having those lunch-time, what-are-we-going-do-when-we-grow-up convos in the ninth grade. I always brag on the two degrees he got while playing football in college.

I have the ultimate winner in my circle of influence…God. I invited him into my circle in August of 2013. He rescued me.

I was damaged from a rough childhood.

When I came to Christ, I started to heal from that damage.

My life is different now. That's because I'm being sharpened by the people in my circle.

Iron Sharpens Iron.

I leave you with two things.

1. Reject negative people and environments. Cut them off or leave those environments if you must.

2. Surround yourself with people who are Striving for Greatness and Living for God.

God Bless, Jeremiah

02/21/16

Sunday's Reflection: "Serve Others…Serve God"

As I took my "Walk With God", I thought about that if you serve others…you serve God.

Monday, my co-workers asking me what I'd do to celebrate my birthday

I responded: Write a column. That was my birthday present to myself. The column got 520 likes. I guess it was a wise decision. ☺

It's amazing how much I love writing now. That wasn't always the case, although God was trying to tell me that it was my gift my whole life.

The first time it was evident was when I was in fifth grade. My teacher asked our class to write about our role models. I wrote about my mom. I won the contest and a free meal at Applebee's. Years passed, and I had a writing assignment for a history class in college. The professor was so impressed by my writing style that he asked me to switch majors to History. I was like, nah, I don't want to teach (Ironic, huh.).

Then I went through something in college that was stressful. A friend said I should write to get my thoughts out. It was therapeutic. I started to write about any and everything. People liked my little Facebook Notes. Apparently, I was deep. ☺

Still, I didn't want to write professionally or anything.

I had an opportunity to write for my hometown newspaper. Still, it wasn't what I wanted to do. I worked for a scouting service and got to evaluate talent and cover my school: Mississippi State.

I liked doing a radio show and evaluating talent. It was fun. I wrote some, but I still saw no redeeming value in it.

But Bill Buckley, a spiritual mentor, affirmed me in my writing. Thanks Mr.Bill.

Fast forward a couple of years, I had a chance to interview Quinton Wesley or "Kirkwood." Because of a college incident, he was viewed as a bad guy to some.

After posting his story, there were so many people showing him love. At that moment, I realized that writing was what I wanted to do. My writing evolved.

God was revealing my gift the whole time. I wouldn't listen, though.

He had to keep putting me through trials to make me realize my purpose.

For me to take to the next level as a writer, I had to grow.

Going through everything I did last year, I was forced to. Those trials birth Sunday Reflections.

Through my Reflections, I encourage people. It gives me another reason to get up.

This week, a co-worker asked me: "What do I consider a successful life?"

I responded: "I want to impact lives."

That's what I was put on this earth to do.

Friday night, God spoke to me in a dream.

In the dream, I was riding in a van. I slipped and gave into one of my demons. Shortly after, the vehicle crashed and started to turn over. The van door opened, and I was able to get out unscathed. But the vehicle turned over and all the other passengers died.

I saw four body bags.

How I interpret the dream? God's trying to tell me that other people's lives are in my hands. I can't lead them the wrong way or stumble. I must keep watch. I must stay diligent in The Word. I have no choice. That's what he's charged me to do.

He wants me to Serve Others. Through Serving Others, I serve him.

I leave you with two things.

1. What's your spiritual gift?

2. If you know what your spiritual gift is, are you using it to serve others?

God Bless, Jeremiah

02/28/16

Sunday's Reflection: "Strive For Unity"

As I took my "Walk With God", I thought how we must strive for unity.

Two events from last Sunday come to mind.

The first was a "Domain Luncheon" at my church. My domain was Education. We discussed how the church could reach minority students.

The second was my school's softball team's games. We lost both. But it was amazing to see most of the people who signed up there. We had such a great time.

At school the next day, everyone was dapping each other up and talking about the game. It was so cool. For a school that relies on everyone working well together, it's nice to have something that engenders camaraderie.

Both events were great. But I didn't know exactly what God was trying to tell me.

Do I talk about diversity in the church or something else?

God always reveals, though. There was a bothersome situation at my other job. And the word that came to mind was…Unity.

If you don't have unity, it disturbs everything.

I'd love to say that the situation got worked out. But it didn't.

My spirits were raised Friday night, though. I had an opportunity to watch Tony Dungy speak. It was one of those great life moments.

Saturday, I was still in a funk. At one point, I put my phone on Airplane mode to block out the world.

I got out of my funk, though.

What got me out of my funk?

Friday, I attended my Club Rewind babies Texans' dance. I was honored that they wanted me to come. My heart was warmed toward the end of the dance.

When the teacher asked the kids grab someone important to them, one of my kids grabbed me. I could believe I was that important to her.

Reflecting on that moment, I remembered what's important and why I value Unity. I must strive to have it in every area of my life.

To achieve it, I must remember what's important…My Why's.

Strive For Unity.

I leave you with two things.

1. Is there unity in all your personal, professional and spiritual relationships?

2. If there isn't unity, what can You do to achieve it?

God Bless, Jeremiah

03/06/16

Sunday's Reflection: "Don't Doubt Yourself"

As I took my "Walk With God", I thought about how we don't need to doubt ourselves.

This week, I had a conversation with a friend.

The friend told me that she was hesitant to do something, because she was too "Shy." I told her not worry about what others have to say and to have confidence. But she shared that she lacked it.

It hurt me to hear that.

But it's amazing how God talks to you. Someone doubted me this week. I proved them wrong. They doubted me nonetheless.

I've always had doubters.

Example: My goal this school year was to improve and mentally prepare myself to step into a classroom next year as the Teacher, not as the assistant.

An administrator told me that they worried that I couldn't because of my "decision-making." It burned that someone would say that. I was like, I got you.

So, as I prepared to take my Special Education test, a test based on critical-thinking, all I thought about was proving that administrator wrong. It ran through my mind several times. I passed.

Another administrator said that's cool. Now you need to pass your Generalist/Core test. I passed that one, too.

Now what?

Not too long after that, the same administrator who doubted me said that I had really improved, and it shows that everything is slowing down.

That's not the only time I was doubted. As I decided to take my writing more seriously, fans said that I couldn't write and that my grammar was horrible, which it was. I took it as a challenge. I studied and focused on getting better. Now, people praise me for the flow and structure of my columns.

The doubt has been deeper than that. Most of my twenty's I was called lazy, sorry and told that I "didn't want to work." I was even told that I needed to stop writing. The same thing I'm using to spread God's message. I got focused and stepped into what God has for me. Now, all those people can say is: "Keep up the good work."

The biggest doubter in this world is on the inside, though.

Case in point: I used to do a radio show before I came to Houston. There was a time where I had an opportunity to anchor the show or lead discussion. But I was like, nah, I'm better at commentary. No one told me that I couldn't do it. I told me that I couldn't do it. Five years later, I host a show and put the whole thing together.

To be real, though, Jesus had doubters.

What reason do we have to trip?

Don't Doubt Yourself.

I leave you with two things.

1. What's the source of your doubt?

2. Once you identify it, work to eradicate it and step into what God has for you. *God Bless, Jeremiah*

03/13/16

Sunday's Reflection: "It's Not About You"

As I took my Walk With God, I thought how it's not about you.

Last week, I attended Eric Thomas' conference in Houston.

There were so many nuggets to churn on. But three things stuck with me. The first was that he asked everyone in attendance to write down the most important people in their lives.

The second nugget was the story of his right-hand man C.J. giving up his ticket to a big overseas trip so that their video guy Carl could bring his wife…Sacrifice.

The third was that ET asked if we were Being The Best Version of Ourselves…deep.

I was convicted. I had to make some changes.

What could I do?

The background of my phone was a picture of myself at the NCAA Tournament…the classic I'm blowing up pic. But it's selfish. That got changed to a family pic.

Next, I thought of the Mission Trip I'm going on. But it starts before the school year ends. I would have to leave my babies the last week of school…selfish!!! That got changed. I'm finishing the year with my babies.

Then I thought about if I was being the Best Version of Myself. I think I'm doing ok.

But could I do better? Yes.

My kids are disciplined and well-behaved. But I made things more engaging but educational. They took to some of the changes…awesome.

The week was still rough. There were some inter-personal dynamics that were weighing me down, and I found out that I was losing one my babies and possibly another one. My spirits were low.

Thursday night, I had a convo with God about everything that was going on.

He was listening, but I wasn't very obedient. I didn't even want to get up Friday morning. I sulked in the bed for 20 minutes. God still showed me grace.

I looked at my phone. My cousin, Allyson, had sent the family a pic of her baby saying that he looked Aunt Florence. It raised my spirits. I got up.

When I got to school, several people had prayer needs. I felt so horrible. I had to apologize for being so negative all week. And I realized why ET says that we can't have a "Bad Day."

When people depend on you, you can't have one.

God continued to speak to me. My best friend text me that he was going back to school. I was so encouraged.

As I went through my Saturday morning routine, my nerves calmed.

Why? I thought of Monday. I had to miss the first 45 minutes of my shift at work. When I returned to work, I was trying to get my kids in order and one of my babies came up to me and gave me a hug. She missed me.

It's not about my feelings. It's about those who depend on me feelings.

It's Not About You.

I leave you with two things.

1. Who are the most important people to you?
2. Are you living for them or yourself?

God Bless, Jeremiah

03/20/16

Sunday's Reflection: "Make An Adjustment"

As I took my "Walk With God", I thought about how you must make an adjustment.

Monday, I got a little batting practice in with some teammates. I got a few cuts in. On my second round of swings, one of my teammates noticed that I was undercutting the ball. He told me to swing more level. I made the adjustment and started to make better contact.

All it took was a minor adjustment more my swing to improve. It's a nice allegory to life. All it takes is a minor adjustment to improve a situation.

It's something I've learned over the past two years working with kids. There's a lot of trial and error. But mostly, there are series of adjustments.

When dealing with kids, everyone has a different approach. Some are bubbly. Some are strict. I'm authoritative.

How you deal with children can extend to how you deal with adults. It's all in the approach. If I've learned anything the past year, it's that.

With my direct nature, I can come across a bit terse or like a butt hole. But that's not my intention. If you don't know me, then you likely don't know that's not my intention. I've become more understanding of that.

I started to make adjustments. I can still be direct. But I preface the statement first or use the "compliment sandwich."

What's the compliment sandwich? Tell the person something positive about themselves. Then give them your criticism. Then reinforce it with something positive.

If anything, put yourself in the other person's shoes. Do you want someone always telling you what you're doing wrong but not what you're doing right?

We must adjust.

It's hard, though. Because if we admit that we need to make an adjustment, that means we must admit we're wrong. No wants to admit that they don't have all the answers.

But we don't. God's the only person with all the answers.

Make those adjustments and be a true Christian witness.

I leave you with two things.

1. What adjustment could you make?

2. Are you willing to make it?

God Bless, Jeremiah

03/27/16

Sunday's Reflection: "Exercise Caution"

As I took my "Walk with God", I thought about how we must exercise caution.

Last Sunday, I went to lunch and forgot my debit card at the restaurant. I was able to retrieve it. Then later that day I lost my wallet. I was able to find it, as well.

Next day, my gym charged me for a fee that I wasn't made aware of when I signed my agreement. I was able to straighten it out.

Tuesday, I had to get another debit card because an establishment's records had been compromised.

None of these situations are willful bad decisions. But I should have been more conscious of what I was doing and exercised caution. All I had to do was slow down and take my time and I wouldn't have forgot my debit card or lost my wallet.

I love when these little things happen. It's God telling me how I can grow. That's why caution is so important.

You must be conscious of everything you do. You must take your time and think before you make decisions.

And you must be conscious of what you put into your spirit. The books you read. The music you listen to. The people and environments you're around. All of it matters.

Please exercise caution.

I leave you with two things.

1. Do you exercise enough caution?

2. What area could you exercise more caution?

God Bless, Jeremiah

04/03/16

Sunday's Reflection: "Don't Be Afraid"

As I took my "Walk With God", I thought about Pastor Steve's Easter sermon: "Don't Be Afraid."

Before I came to Christ, I was afraid. Afraid of Greatness.

People told me that I had a world of "potential." It was evident. In elementary school, I was the number one kid in my class. I was in the gifted program. The potential for greatness was there. I cared more about video games and sports, though.

My mom used to say: "If you cared about school like you cared about sports, then you would be a straight-A student. It would go in one ear and out the other. I just wanted to play *Goldeneye* and *WrestleMania* all day with my friends.

Heck, my talent for words was always there. A friend once told me: "Man, Moot you be saying real stuff…It's just the way you say it." I never looked at it as a talent.

Instead of wasting time in college, I should have been honing that talent. I should have been building my dynasty, not one on NCAA Football.

I didn't want people expecting something from me. That's some scary stuff. I didn't want to deal with the pressure that comes with being Great.

God meant for me to be Great. I shouldn't have been afraid. None of should be.

To those that are afraid, don't be.

Don't be afraid of constructive criticism. You might grow.

Don't be afraid of your past. Use it as a testimony. I don't care if you committed a crime. I don't care if you were a dog or a hoe. I don't care if you were an alcoholic, gambler or addicted to drugs.

God can use you. He used Abraham. He was a liar. He used Moses. He stuttered and was a murderer. He used David. He was an adulterer and committed first-degree murder. Solomon, the wisest man that ever lived, was a "womanizer."

Don't be afraid to be more successful than your friends and family. If that's what God has for you, then that's what he has for you.

Don't be afraid to use your gift. It was given to you for a reason.

Don't be afraid to be yourself. God made you that way.

Ultimately, don't be afraid to Trust God and his plan for your life.

I'm not afraid anymore. You shouldn't be, either. God got you.

Don't Be Afraid.

I leave you with two things.

1. What are you afraid of?

2. If you stopped being afraid, what would happen to your life or those around you lives?

God Bless, Jeremiah

04/10/16

Sunday's Reflection: "Carry Yourself Properly"

As I took my "Walk With God", I thought about a speech from Eric Thomas.

In the speech, he told a group of students to "Take Yourself Seriously."

He wasn't telling them to be anal, pretentious and to behave like they're better than the next person. He was telling them to carry themselves properly.

That's the gap. We're not expected to take ourselves seriously, even in the Christian community.

It matters how you carry yourself. How you walk, talk and maneuver. Ironing your clothes matters. Your posture matters. If I can look at you and discern that you're a Christian, it matters.

While I was college, a childhood friend told me: "I looked up to you growing up."

Me (In my head): Bruh, what? You picked a fight with me on a regular basis.

That hit me. And it hits me even more now. Someone is always watching.

I watched my Dad. He wasn't perfect. He didn't live in the same house as me. But he was a good father.

What he did show me? He didn't drink much in front of me. He didn't smoke or curse. He dressed well and was always presentable. He was punctual and never unemployed.

He's the classic strong, silent type. I've been told that I'm a lot like him, although I'm more of the strong, hard-to-figure-out type.

He was there at my big events. He was there for the serious moments, as well. When he found out someone tried to sexual assault me in middle school, he didn't give me the macho-dad talk. He talked to me about it.

When my mom was in the hospital, he told me if she didn't make it, then I would stay with him.

When I was racially profiled and in jail for a day and a half, he was ready to tear it down.

My most vivid memory, though, of my dad was when he called me on my 21st birthday and left a voicemail. He repeatedly stated how much he loved me. It blew my mind. I knew my dad loved me. But that was real.

Most importantly, my dad modeled what a man is supposed to be. He carried himself properly.

I try to be like my dad. I try to be consistent, loving and always there. Someone is watching.

That's what God calls us to do.

To Carry Ourselves Properly.

I leave you with two things.

1. Do you carry yourself properly?

2. Who's watching the way you carry yourself?

God Bless, Jeremiah

04/17/16

Sunday's Reflection: "Be Good Stewards"

As I took my "Walk With God", I thought about a book: "The Wealthy Barber."

It was a phenomenal read. In the book, a barber, Roy, doles out financial advice.

The book isn't Christian based, but it can apply to Christian life--Roy preached good stewardship.

As Christians, we're charged to be financially healthy.

The book was a good reference material for someone like me. I'm in the "Saving Stage" of financial planning.

I'm thankful to be in this stage, because I've had my struggles. Once, I had a decision: pay rent or fix my car. It wasn't the best feeling. I've been evicted and faced homelessness.

Even with that, I made poor financial decisions. When I got my first apartment in Houston, I rented a flat-screen TV. I didn't need it. But I wanted it. The money I should have been saving went to a TV…dumb.

In college, I got "student refund" checks. Instead of buying all my books or saving some of it, I used the money to buy video games and clothes.

I have regrets from college. I should have read more, wrote more and had a better circle of influence.

My biggest regret is not developing financial literacy and health.

I've learned from those mistakes. And because I've learned from those mistakes, I can be a blessing to others.

I love being able to do things for my kids and others.

It comes with sacrifice. There are times I want to stunt, hang or, "have a life."

But to quote Dave Ramsey: "I want to live like no one else, so I can live like no one else."

Be A Good Steward.

I leave you with two things.

1. Are you a good steward?

2. If not, what can you do to become a better steward?

God Bless, Jeremiah

04/24/16

Sunday's Reflection: "Take Refuge In Him"

As I took my "Walk With God", I thought about the storm that devastated Houston.

People lost their lives, homes were flooded, and communities were destroyed.

School was cancelled all week.

I got some reading and writing done. But I wasn't locked in. I was thinking about an upcoming Career Fair. I'm stressing over it. Its pressure that's understandable but with parts of the city under water, it's selfish to worry about

After I had lunch with a friend, my spirits were lifted.

Saturday, I had a calming moment. As the sun beamed down, I realized that God was shining on the city. He brought us through the storm. The citizen of Houston banded together and supported each other. No one complained about what they'd lost. They put a smile on their faces and started the process of rebuilding the city.

Psalms 18:2 is a great scripture on which to meditate: *"The LORD is my rock and my fortress and my deliverer, My God, my rock, in whom I take refuge; my shield and the horn of my salvation, my stronghold."*

Houston, we've seen devastation but remember: God is there for us...Take Refuge in Him.

I leave you with two things.

1. Has there been a time when you didn't take refuge in God?

2. If you didn't, why didn't you take refuge in him?

God Bless, Jeremiah

05/01/16

Sunday's Reflection: "Put Your Faith In God, Not People"

As I took my "Walk With God", I thought about how you must put your faith in God, not people.

Monday, I was betrayed by a person who I put faith in. I was angry. I couldn't function. I got less than two hours of sleep.

Reflecting on that day, I remembered what Pastor Brand said years ago: *"Never put your faith in people, they will ALWAYS disappoint you."*

I expected to have a bad week. But it wasn't. My kids were good and enjoyed their lesson of the week: Rapport.

In addition to that, I got encouragement from co-workers and friends, which really helped.

On Wednesday, I had a good day at work and looked impressive in front of administrators--receiving praise for my performance.

I'm not big on affirmation, but it felt kind of good, and I kind of needed it--especially considering I had my first Career Fair the next day.

Due to nervousness, I couldn't sleep that night. My nerves were calmed by others praying for me.

When I got to the Career Fair, it didn't feel overwhelming. I got out there and sold myself. I couldn't stop talking. One school seemed very interested and gave me the "business card."

That felt good. I may not get to interview with that school, but it felt good to be wanted.

The next day, I found out that my kids were disciplined and behaved without me there.

After I got off work, things were put into perspective. I got a call from Aunt Linda. Derrick, my older cousin had lost his battle with Sickle Cell Anemia.

I was angry most of the week, but I should have been thankful for God has given me.

He's given me kids to pour into. He's blessed me with good health. He's blessed me with life. God doesn't have to give me any of those things.

God knew I needed. I was down and got constant encouragement.

Also, he reminded me that he was in control, not me.

I must put my faith in him, not people.

I leave you with two things.

1. Have you ever put too much faith in another person?

2. How did God remind you that you did?

God Bless, Jeremiah

05/08/16

Sunday's Reflection: "Take The Log Out Of Your Eye"

As I took my "Walk With God" this morning, I thought about how you must take the log out of your eye. Two situations illustrated that.

First Situation

My kids were in the gym, and one of my girls was playfully hitting the other kids too much. I asked her to stop twice.

After the third time, I called her over. Before I got the words out, she said: "I know I'm hitting too many people today."

She didn't do it again. She was accountable.

Second Situation

I was waiting to watch Captain America: Civil War. Two people asked if someone was saving seats next to me. I said no. But someone was saving seats.

A man was very upset and started berating them. They were restrained and didn't engage. Eventually, they changed seats and the man sat. (Not before cursing them out one last time.)

In the first situation, the nine-year old child took accountability. In the second, the middle-age man couldn't realize the error of his ways or "take the log out of his own eye."

As Christians, we need to be like that nine-year-old and not the middle-aged man.

Take the log out of your eye.

I leave you with two things.

1. Do you have a time where you didn't take the log out of your eye?

2. If you had, would the situations had turned out better?

God Bless, Jeremiah

05/15/16

Sunday's Reflection: "Christ Cleans Out Your Bucket"

As I took my "Walk With God", I thought about how Christ cleans out your bucket.

Sunday, I celebrated Mother's Day with my family. Listening to the family secrets, I was like, whoa, this is what I come from. But my own life has been crazy.

When I gave my life to Christ, it stopped being crazy. He cleaned out my bucket.

How does he clean out of bucket?

Bishop McCarter, a pastor in Crawford, Mississippi, had a Great illustration of it. He took out bucket filled with dirt and then took out pitcher with clean water. He poured the clean water in the bucket. The more clean water he poured into it…the clearer the water got.

That's what Christ does. He cleans out our bucket little by little.

When we first give our life to Christ, we're babes. With awareness, though, we get convicted. We become careful about what we watch, the people we're around, the environments we're in and how we deal with situations.

As a result, we have more peace. I know I have more of it. Relationships have been restored. I'm growing. My spirit is calmer.

Last weekend, someone said: "You're in a different space."

I am. God has "cleaned out my bucket."

I leave you with two things.

1. Have you fully accepted Christ?

2. If you do, he'll clean out your bucket, too.

God Bless, Jeremiah

05/22/16

Sunday's Reflection: "Let Nothing Steal Your Joy"

As I took my "Walk With God", I thought about how you should let nothing steal your joy.

Monday, I was in a good mood. My kids even commented that I was in a good mood. I ended up getting some troubling news, which killed that vibe.

Good week gone bad.

After talking to a friend, though, my thought process changed. The friend said: "The week would be what I make it."

My mind was eased by those words.

Everything came into sync Friday. We have "Fun Fridays" at my school. My kids decided it was a good idea to chase me and spray me with water bottles. It was fun. But it also a reminder as to who is important to me…my babies.

Saturday morning, I was glad that I had a good week. It could have gone bad, but I made a conscious choice to make it good.

We can't let anything distract us from our mission. If we lose sight of that, we lose our joy.

Let Nothing Steal Your Joy.

I leave you with two things.

1. Do you sweat the small stuff?

2. Is it stealing your joy?

God Bless, Jeremiah

05/29/16

Sunday's Reflection: "Be A Part Of The Solution, Not The Problem"

As I took my "Walk With God", I thought about how you must be a part of the solution, not the problem.

This week, Problems arose. But in every situation, I had a solution or was part of it.

Someone questioned my leadership. Instead of overreacting and being insecure, I weathered the storm and grew from it.

A storm hit Houston. As a result, my Club Rewind program understaffed. Instead of complaining, we held it together and made sure things ran smooth.

I learned about myself and leadership through these situations. I learned that sometimes you must suck up your ego. Sometimes you're going to be challenged. And sometimes you must forget your differences with others and work together.

Leadership isn't about proving how smart you are or proving how much of a big shot that you are. It's about sacrifice.

My kids are at the forefront of every decision I make. They don't like me being gone for five minutes. So, before I make a move, I think about how it will affect them.

As I grow as a leader, that mind set must extend to every person I lead.

When faced with a decision, you must ask yourself the question: Is what I'm tripping on going to hurt the group?

If it does, then don't do it.

It's easier said than done--especially for me. I've always had a BIG mouth.

In 2010, Mississippi State lost a football game to Auburn. I was upset by the loss. I blamed it on a quarterback controversy. I favored one quarterback.

After the game, I attacked the other quarterback via social media. It caused problems.

A childhood friend, Davarus, gave me a call and held me accountable for it. I removed the post. The damage had been done, though. I was wrong. I was part of problem, not the solution.

Christians must strive to be the solution in a situation. You never want to be part of the problem.

The solution to a problem isn't always simple. You might have to suck up your ego. You might have to address a conflict. You might have to say you're WRONG.

Examples: Sibling rivalry, personality clashes at work, parental disagreement over discipline, direction of a company or Church.

In Ecclesiastes 8:5-8, Solomon writes: *"Whoever keeps a command will know no evil thing, and the wise heart will know the proper time and the just way. For there is a time and a way for everything, although man's trouble lies heavy on him. For he does not know what is to be, for who can tell him how it will be? No man has power to retain the spirit, or power over the day of death. There is no discharge from war, nor will wickedness deliver those who are given to it."*

Translation: Even though we might want to complain or kick up a stink, we need to keep God first in all our decisions and make sure what you're doing is proper for the time.

Be A Part Of The Solution, Not The Problem.

I leave you with two things.

1. Have you ever been part of the problem?

2. Do you wish you had come up with the solution first?

God Bless, Jeremiah

06/05/16

Sunday's Reflection: Time to "Fly"

As I sit and reflect on the week, I thought about how it's time to fly.

Last Sunday. After two and half years as an assistant, I was told that I'd get my own classroom in the Children's ministry.

On Tuesday, I received a good work evaluation--up .8 points from the previous year…improvement.

On Wednesday, things exploded. I had a screening interview with Human Resources of a school district. The interview went well. So well that schools from across the district started blowing me up to set up interviews. I set up three.

I didn't anticipate one school wanting me to come in that day. I decided to go to the interview last minute. The interview was amazing. I felt good about my chances. My feeling was correct. The principal called me shortly after I arrived home and offered me the position.

It was a surreal moment. I accepted. I had no reason to hesitate. I was sold during the interview when the principal told me that "they're not ducks…they're eagles…eagles soar."

That's what I want to do.

The best feeling was sharing the news with friends, family, co-workers and my babies. Telling my babies was bitter-sweet, but I was glad I got to share that moment with them.

After saying goodbye to my babies, I hopped on a plane to Monterrey, Mexico. It was time to do the Lord's work. I soaked it all in the first day with Team USA. The team has so much camaraderie and a thirst for Christ.

Team USA were champions in victory. They not only won the game, but they prayed and shared the word with Team China.

With all the blessings the Lord was sending my way, I had to pause and truly reflect on the journey God had put me through the past two years.

My first year in education was tumultuous. Everything that could go wrong did. My Aunt Florence died, and I wasn't even allowed to process it. I lived with a roommate who was a little racially biased--to put it mildly. My church group split. My dwell group split and eventually dismantled.

Following that year, I knew I had to make some changes, although some thought I was already going in the right direction. I don't subscribe to others standard for me, though. There was a gap I had to close and damage I had to repair.

In my second year, things started to come into focus. Everything slowed down. I started to come into my own.

Relationships that were broken have been restored. I can't explain how it feels to have a great relationship with my big brother again. We used to be tight. Then we didn't talk much for ten years. We fought--literally and figuratively. Now, we talked about self-improvement and books.

Nothing but God!!!

Those who doubted me either praise me or have nothing to say.

I've been encouraged throughout the year by those who are encouraged by me. They gave me a reason to pop up in the morning.

It's not that I didn't face challenges. That changed the last month of the year. I was under attacked at work. All I heard was negativity and, at times, was harassed. I started to get up a little slower.

Despite end of year challenges, the year culminated with the next phase of my life clearer. I'm so excited for the next step. I get to combine my two passions: kids and writing.

It's a dream come true.

My road has been a long one. I sulked for years wanting more love from my mom. I was losing at life.

Now, I'm winning at life, at peace and ready to step into what God has for me.

Last Sunday, someone said that it was time for me to "Fly."

I agree.

It's time that I do.

I leave you with two things.

1. Are you ready to take the next step?

2. If you're ready to, giving your life to Christ is the only way that will happen.

God Bless, Jeremiah

Conclusion

Sunday's Reflection: Going Into The "Big World"

As I took my "Walk With God", I thought about my last day at "The Carlton Center" and Cypress Fairbanks School District.

I think of the evolution that I've gone through as an employee of the school district.

My first year was horrible. I made several mistakes, exhibited poor composure and experienced system overload due to my introverted nature. I didn't know protocol or how to be a professional.

I questioned my path.

Did I have what it took to be a Teacher? I didn't know the answer.

While I was considering teaching Elementary, I didn't know it was the proper direction.

Ann Scott, who I worked under my first year, told me to not think that way…It was nothing but "The Devil."

I had to trust God.

Trusting him, I turned down a newspaper writing position. It's not what God wanted for me. It wasn't easy to turn down. My goal is to write professionally and to write books. But I wanted to work with kids.

The move proved prescient. After pushing through the first-year storms, it all came to pass my second year. Everything slowed down. I got my temperament under control, learned protocol and how to be a professional.

I found my groove.

By February, I was ready to teach. Someone thought I was and hired me. A year after turning down a writing offer, I was offered a job teaching it.

Look at God.

Paul writes in 1 Corinthians 13:11: *"When I was a child, I spoke like a child, I thought like a child, I reasoned like a child. When I became a man, I gave up childish ways."*

The man that was once childish in his ways is going into the "Big World."

I leave you with one thing.

1. Push through the storms, because there's a rainbow on the other side.

God Bless, Jeremiah

Acknowledgements

My turnaround would not have been possible without my Carlton Center family. They mentored and helped me navigate the stormy waters. They were patient with my fidgety, aloof, "bougie" ways.

The "Carlton Prayer Group" helped me get through so many trials. I had the pleasure of leading the group my second year.

Rhonda Turns, my principal, was always a valuable resource. She helped me with my resume and gave me tips for interviews. She did so knowing that I was planning on leaving the school to work at the Elementary level.

I'll be forever grateful.

The office personnel are the unsung heroes of any school. They always helped me when I needed something--big or small. I truly appreciate them.

I'll never forget the parting gifts and words of wisdom given to me on my final day. I felt the love from the Carlton staff. I love them, too. I will miss them.

The Carlton reared me. But I started Club Rewind, a Cy-Fair before and after-care program, the summer before I started at The Carlton.

I'd never worked with kids before I started the job. I didn't know if I'd enjoy it. I didn't even know how to work with them. I did learn and started to love it. They became my life.

My kid's little notes and energetic spirits always brought a smile to my face.

The past year at A.Robison was particularly wonderful. I learned so much from the teachers on the campus. I had an opportunity to observe a few of them for my certification. A.Robison is one of the best schools in Cy-Fair. I'll be able to use some of skills that I learned from those teachers in my own career. Thank you ladies.

My A.Rob babies made the year special. They allowed me to grow, experiment and love on them.

The most memorable moment of every week was the announcement of the "Star Student." The kids would literally pester me to see who won from the previous week. I fondly remember one of my students opining "I knew it" when I announced one of his classmates as the winner.

They loved my themed days and had fun with my "lesson of the week." I felt like a proud papa when I found out that my kids were showing appreciation to their parents, teachers and administrators after I asked them to as a lesson.

Not only did my kids respect me, but they challenged and helped me grow as a leader.

One of my kids chastised me, saying "I don't ever play with the kids." I realized I needed to do more. I started to interact more and played tag with kids on "Fun Fridays."

When I got to loud once, one of my kids asked why am I getting all "police officer?" I knew I had to speak in a softer tone.

My baby girls taught me what "Shopkins" were. Those things are impossible to find.☺

My babies valued me. They asked where I was at when I wasn't there, even if it was for 15 minutes. When I missed work to attend the Career Fair, I asked one of my kids how it was in my absence. She said it was ok…except for everyone "flapping their gums about you."

Also, they invited me to their events and were always happy to see me, although it wasn't always "chit-chat with Mr. Jeremiah time."

I love my little "Avengers." What I'd do to be able to say "Assemble" one last time.

I'll miss my babies. I have new babies to pour into, though. I must give them my all.

To Cy-Fair, Thank you and goodbye…for now.

God Bless, Jeremiah

www.ingramcontent.com/pod-product-compliance
Lightning Source LLC
Chambersburg PA
CBHW042305150426
43197CB00001B/15